The Mouse-de
and the Crocodiles

A Folk Tale from Malaysia

Retold by Beverley Randell   Illustrated by Pat Reynolds

Once upon a time,
a small animal
called a mouse-deer
lived in a forest.

He was only as big as a rabbit,
but he made up for being small
by being very cheeky.
He often tricked
the other animals
because he liked getting
his own way.

One day, the mouse-deer
saw some red fruit
growing on a tree
on the far side of a river.
The fruit looked delicious.

"I wonder how I can get
across the river?"
the mouse-deer asked himself.
"It is full of crocodiles.
They will grab me
and eat me.
I must trick them."

The mouse-deer
stopped to think
how he could do it.

5

Then the mouse-deer
smiled to himself.

"Crocodiles! Crocodiles!
Come here!" he called.
"You must all do what I say,
because I work for the king."

"The king has told me
to count you,"
said the mouse-deer.
"He needs to know
how many crocodiles
live in this river."

The crocodiles
were scared of the king!
They swam towards
the mouse-deer,
and waited in a line
to be counted.

The crocodiles
were so close together
that their backs made a bridge
across the river.

"That's good," said the mouse-deer.
"Now keep still
while I count you.
If you move,
I'll just have to start counting
all over again."

The mouse-deer raced quickly
along the backs of the crocodiles.
He counted as he ran.
"Two, four, six, eight, ten, **twelve**,"
he shouted as he hurried across.

And when he jumped off
the last crocodile,
he was on the other side of the river!

The mouse-deer turned around
and laughed at the crocodiles.
"Ha, ha, ha!
I don't work for the **king**!
I tricked you that time," he said.
"You have just made
a bridge for me!"

And he skipped away
on his thin little legs,
laughing as he went.

This made the crocodiles angry.
They opened their jaws,
and showed their sharp teeth.

"Just you wait, you cheeky thing!"
they called after him.
"We will catch you
the next time you try
to drink from the river.
We will catch you,
sooner or later.
Just you wait and see!"

But the mouse-deer didn't care
one little bit.
He was too busy eating
the delicious red fruit.
He knew that he could trick
the crocodiles again
if he had to!